MrDeadletters

2020-2023

A curated collection of

love and erotic inspired micropoetry

Vol. 1 Ed. 1

MRDEADLETTERS VOL I EDITION, NOVEMBER 2023

Copyright 2023 © by Michael D. Dennis

All rights reserved under the Pan-American Copyright Conventions.
Published in the United States by Ocean Street Press.

All rights reserved. No part of this publication can be reproduced or transmitted in any form or by any means, electronic or mechanical, without permission in writing from the author or publisher.

Ocean Street Press
ISBN-10: 0-9960964-4-2
ISBN-13: 978-0-9960964-4-7 (Hardcover)
ISBN-13: 978-0-9960964-7-8 (Paperback)
LCCN: 2023919831

Ocean Street Press
Author's web address www.michaelddennis.com

Printed in the United States of America

Cover Art: Austin Maples

10 30 12 6 1 9

First Edition

For my Kitty Kat who keeps my lover's heart dreaming.

two souls that
suffered apart
together turn
into one that is
unbreakable

i want to
be the
greatest
risk of
your life

i want to hold
your heart like
a work of art

i'm easy
to love
impossible
to forget

i will lick you
until you have
nothing left inside
and only the look
of satisfaction
in your eyes

you > everything

you are my kind
of one of a kind

memories of
you are
tattooed
on my skin
permanent
signs of our
lover's sins

let me...

undress you
obsess over you
and use my tongue
to caress you

subdue me
+
consume me

"give it to me"

she handed me
her heart and now
we'll never be apart

fuck away my pain
until it's gone
and we feel insane

i'll ignite the
flame that
burns inside
you when
you say my
name and i'm
behind you

give me your
everything and
i'll be your forever

when i call you
mine and see
you smile it
makes me love
you wild

i need to hear
your dirty words
in my ear tell
me your desires
without any fear

make me
climax in
my heart
and then
our love
will never
break apart

let me lift up
your skirt from
behind slide your
panties to the side
so you can feel
pleasure deep inside

we should never
wake up from
this obscene dream

"i need to feel you"

i went deeper
inside than she
ever imagined

i was broken
and torn apart
you saved me
and turned my
chaos into art

when i'm inside
you i feel the
pulse of your
heart on my
cock and i
can't stop

lick me when i
drip for you and
i promise i'll
submit to you

be my whore
and beg me
to fuck you
on the floor
until you can't
take anymore

it's your smile
that drives me
so madly wild

tie me to
the bed
and lick
me until
i'm dead

the world
disappears
whenever
you're near

love me for my
mind and even
more for the
way i fuck you
from behind

it's your heart
that seduced
me but your
body that i
want to use me

i want to choke
on your cum
down in my soul
until it's all i know

my heart is yours
until the end
the end is never
and you are my
forever

my tongue is
your personal
sex toy you
can ride it
in all the ways
you enjoy

if it hurts
just hold me
tighter it's in
the darkness
that you'll
see me shine

you light that
fire inside my
soul the one
that i can't
control

seduce my mind
and you will find
that i'll pleasure
you for a lifetime

the taste of
your pussy
lips intoxicates
me so deeply
my soul can't
resist it

the most beautiful
view is the one that
starts with you

fuck me
with your
tongue and
kiss my lips
when your
done

hold me naked
in the darkness
and i'll fill you
with my light

you make
it impossible
to leave you
are the air
that i breathe

get on your
knees like
you're saying
a prayer and
i'll fill your
mouth and pull
your hair

kiss me like you
are going to
consume my soul

dreamers like us
never die we fly
so high because
love's secret is in
our eyes

you are the
one that i
adore let me
make you my
personal whore

your dirty smile
intoxicates me
with every inhale
driving me wild

let's never
come back
down from
our castle
in the clouds

i'd cut out my
heart to give
to you because
it belongs to you

some days are
made to just
lay in bed
naked with you

my tongue
sucks and
licks your
clit until
you cum
and submit
to my worship

love isn't cruel
when it's true
believe me
because it's
different with you

my heart is yours
forever let's never
stop this adventure

once i fill you
with my seed
this life together
is ours forever

you are the only
one it was you
only you all along

i don't want to
watch porn i
want to make
one with you

if your heart
is broken i will
kiss every piece
and put you back
together

only fuck me
if eternity is
long enough
to love me

seduce me
and use me
just make sure
you kiss me
when you're
through with me

you are
such a
rare find
i need you
until the
end of time

let's get crazy
and pretend
to make a baby

i see you
everywhere
because you
are my
everything